*The*

# JAREDITES

*The*

*Mark E. Petersen*

**Deseret Book**
Salt Lake City, Utah

Note: The author wishes to make clear that this is not an official publication of The Church of Jesus Christ of Latter-day Saints. The opinions and views expressed are the author's, for which he alone is responsible.

# CONTENTS

# Chapter 1

# A HIDDEN PEOPLE

The Jaredite nation is unknown in world history to any but Latter-day Saints. It was hidden by the Almighty from all other peoples. Its life span probably covered nearly twenty centuries, from shortly after the Flood to possibly 400 to 500 B.C.

This mysterious people left their mark on two hemispheres and produced populations of untold millions. They originated in a heavenly miracle and expired in degradation and civil war. An early American nation for most of its existence, its roots went back to the Tower of Babel in ancient Mesopotamia, affirming that there was such a tower, despite the doubts of some scholars. These people came from it!

There was a confounding of the languages there also. These Jaredites lived through it, although their own speech was not affected.

And there *was* a dispersion by divine decree. These people took an important part in it. Like later dispersions, it grew out of wickedness, a senseless rebellion against God. Jared and his family were exceptions, however. In this dispersion they were moved from Babel to the choicest land on earth, because they loved the Lord and sought to serve him.

But God had placed firm conditions on the occupancy of that promised land. He pronounced both a blessing and a curse upon it. If those dwelling there would serve the Lord, he would prosper them. If they rebelled against him, they would face the threat of utter destruction. This is a lesson that the Jaredite nation never learned.

At various periods in their lives they enjoyed the rich fruits of obedience, but when sin finally triumphed, they collapsed in the throes of corruption and rebellion. They should have known—we all should understand—that no person or nation can fight God and win.

Theirs was a suicidal history. When at last they turned completely away from the Lord, they fell under his threat of certain destruction. Their fratricidal wars wiped out every family and every city—men, women, and children alike—leaving not a semblance of life to tell the tale.

The last survivor was the king himself, and he lived only long enough to see his realm decimated in wars. He died with nothing but a desperate memory of what it once was and a lingering glimpse of what it might have been.

This ancient nation dwelt in America for possibly two millennia, totally undiscovered by the rest of the world. It was born by itself, lived by itself, and died by itself. It had no foreign foe and suffered no attack from without.

The Jaredites sowed and nurtured the seeds of their own destruction. Yet over the years came periods of great prosperity when they became very wealthy and built many cities as they spread out in the land. They had productive mines of gold, silver, and other metals, and they trafficked in many forms of manufactured goods.

At times the Jaredites were granted some of the most remarkable spiritual manifestations known to man. No nation ever had greater promise for the future.

But dying by its own hand, the Jaredite nation moldered into dust, unseen, unheralded, unmourned, the price of rebellion against the God of this land who had personal relationships with its leaders but whom they subsequently refused to serve.

The eventual discovery of the Jaredite remains came by sheer accident, years after the final call to battle faded into silence. The Lord had brought to this continent another people who established a city called Zarahemla and also colonized much of the surrounding area. One group built a city deep in the wilderness. After some years of isolation they yearned to return to their relatives and friends in Zarahemla, but they had forgotten the way back. Though they sent out an expedition to determine the direction to travel, it failed. In its journey, however, the search party came upon the last battleground of the Jaredites. All members of the party were appalled at what they saw.

The expedition, after traveling through a region of "many waters," discovered "a land which was covered with bones of men, and of beasts, and was also covered with ruins of buildings of every kind, having discovered a land which had been peopled with a people who were as numerous as the hosts of Israel."

To prove that the things they had said were true, they brought back twenty-four plates of gold, filled with engravings, as well as large breastplates of brass and copper, and swords, the blades of which were "cankered with rust." No one in the land was able to interpret the language or the engravings on the plates. (Mosiah 8:8-11.)

Carrying their newfound records with them, the search party returned home. When later this colony did rejoin the people of Zarahemla, their leader, a man named Limhi, delivered the mysterious gold plates to Mosiah, the king of Zarahemla. Mosiah, who also was a prophet, had received from the Lord a Urim and Thummim by which he was able to translate from one language to another.

News of the discovery of the twenty-four plates soon circulated among the people of Zarahemla, and they were "desirous beyond measure to know concerning those people who had been destroyed."

Mosiah translated the records "by the means of those two stones which were fastened into the two rims of a bow. Now these things were prepared from the beginning, and were handed down from generation to generation, for the purpose of interpreting languages; and they have been kept and preserved by the hand of the Lord, that he should discover to every creature who should possess the land the iniquities and abominations of his people; and whosoever has these things is called seer, after the manner of old times.

"Now after Mosiah had finished translating these records, behold, it gave an account of the people who were destroyed, from the time that they were destroyed back to the building of the great tower, at the time the Lord confounded the language of the people and they were scattered abroad upon the face of all the earth, yea, and even from that time back until the creation of Adam.

"Now this account did cause the people of Mosiah to mourn exceedingly, yea, they were filled with sorrow; nevertheless it gave them much knowledge, in the which they did rejoice." (Mosiah 28:2-18.)

The Lord made known the history of the Jaredites to Mosiah's people as a lesson for them in the hope that they would not make the same mistake and rebel against him.

When the prophet Alma later gave these same twenty-four plates to his son Helaman for safekeeping, he explained this fact to him, saying:

"And now, I will speak unto you concerning those twenty-four plates, that ye keep them, that the mysteries and the works of darkness, and their secret works, or the secret works of those people who have been destroyed, may be made manifest unto this people; yea, all their murders, and robbings, and their plunderings, and all their wickedness and abominations, may be made manifest unto this people; yea, and that ye preserve these interpreters.

"For behold, the Lord saw that his people began to work in darkness, yea, work secret murders and abominations; therefore the Lord said, if they did not repent they should be destroyed from off the face of the earth." (Alma 37:21-22.)

These plates had been prepared by a Jaredite prophet named Ether, who, having witnessed the last battles of his people, recorded them on the plates; then he too was taken from the scene. He had fulfilled the Lord's purpose by describing how a mysterious and isolated people had lived through many centuries on the choicest area in the world, only to perish by their own hands.

# Chapter 2

# THE TOWER OF BABEL

**F**ollowing the Flood, the descendants of Noah multiplied rapidly. They drifted east from the resting place of the ark and found a plain in the land of Shinar, where they settled down. The Bible tells us:

"They said one to another, Go to, let us make brick, and burn them throughly. And they had brick for stone, and slime had they for morter.

"And they said, Go to, let us build us a city and a tower, whose top may reach unto heaven; and let us make a name, lest we be scattered abroad upon the face of the whole earth.

"And the Lord came down to see the city and the tower, which the children of men builded. And the Lord said, Behold, the people is one, and they have all one language; and this they begin to do: and now nothing will be restrained from them, which they have imagined to do. Go to, let us go down, and there confound their language, that they may not understand one another's speech.

"So the Lord scattered them abroad from thence upon the face of all the earth: and they left off to build the city. Therefore is the name of it called Babel; because the Lord did there confound the language of all the earth: and from thence did the Lord scatter them abroad upon the face of all the earth." (Genesis 11:2-9.)

In the Prophet Joseph Smith's revision of this passage, the latter part of it reads:

"And the Lord said, Behold the people are the same, and they all have the same language; and this tower they begin to build, and now, nothing will be restrained from them, which they have imagined, except I, the Lord, confound their language, that they may not understand one another's speech. So I, the Lord, will scatter them abroad from thence, upon all the face of the land, and unto every quarter of the earth.

"And they were confounded, and left off to build the city, and they hearkened not unto the Lord, therefore, is the name of it called Babel, because the Lord was displeased with their works, and did there confound the language of all the earth; and from thence did the Lord scatter them abroad upon the face thereof." (JST Genesis 11:5-6.)

In regard to the name Babel, the Jewish Masoretic text says, "Therefore the name of it was called Babel because the Lord there confounded the language of all the earth, and from thence did the Lord scatter them abroad upon the face of all the earth."

The rendering by the Roman Catholic Jerusalem Bible is very interesting:

"Throughout the earth men spoke the same language, with the same vocabulary. Now as they moved eastward they found a plain in the land of Shinar where they settled. They said to one another, 'Come, let us make bricks and bake them in the fire.'—For stone they used bricks, and for mortar they used bitumen.—'Come,' they said, 'let us build ourselves a town and a tower with its top reaching heaven. Let us make a name for ourselves, so that we may not be scattered about the whole earth.

"Now Yahweh came down to see the town and the tower that the sons of man had built. 'So they are all a single people with a single language!' said Yahweh. 'This is but the start of their undertakings! There will be nothing too hard for them to do. Come, let us go down and confuse their language on the spot so that they can no longer understand one another.' Yahweh scattered them thence over the whole face of the earth, and they stopped building the town. It was named Babel therefore, because there Yahweh confused the language of the whole earth. It was from there that Yahweh scattered them over the whole face of the earth."

The name Babylon is derived from Babel. Well-known

throughout both modern and ancient scripture, it is synonymous with evil, confusion, and "the great and abominable church."

The ancient city of Babylon supposedly was located beside the Euphrates River about 55 miles south of modern Baghdad. It is believed to have existed from the fourth millennium B.C. Under Hammurabi (1950 B.C.), the old Babylonian empire reached its zenith.

The plain of Shinar, where the tower was built, is sometimes called the plains of Babylonia.

Zikkurats, or stage towers, were characteristic features of the architecture of both Assyria and Babylonia in ancient times. Ruins of such towers have been found at Borsippa, near what is believed to be the site of old Babylon. Efforts have been made through tradition to associate these ruins with the tower of Babel, but such efforts have been unsuccessful.

There are other points of interest in the related scriptures. In Genesis, some passages use a plural form in reference to the acts of God. For example, God said, "Let *us* make man in our image, after *our* likeness." (Genesis 1:26.)

Following the fall of Adam, he spoke, saying, "Behold, he is become as one of *us*." (Genesis 3:22.)

Similarly, regarding the Tower of Babel he declared, "Let *us* go down, and there confound their language." (Genesis 11:7.) Note the plural form that is used.

In the Book of Abraham we also find the plural form in the description of the various steps in creation: "And then the Lord said: Let us go down. And they went down at the beginning, and they, that is the Gods, organized and formed the heavens and the earth. And they (the Gods) said: Let there be light; and there was light. And they (the Gods) comprehended the light, for it was bright; and they divided the light, or caused it to be divided, from the darkness." (Abraham 4:1, 3-4.)

This plural form appears throughout Abraham's record of creation.

Note now how the Prophet Joseph Smith shed light on this matter. In his revision of the fall of Adam, we read: "And I the

Lord God said unto mine Only Begotten, Behold, the man is become as one of us." (JST Genesis 3:28.) The mystery of the plural form is solved, and the language used regarding Babel becomes quite clear.

Since all versions of the Bible give essentially the same information as the King James Translation, and since the Book of Mormon provides adequate corroboration to the account, there is little if any reason for the believer in Holy Writ to doubt the story of Babel. There was such a tower, and there was a confusion of tongues in connection with it. The hundreds of languages and dialects existing today give evidence of it.

There was also a dispersion of the descendants of Noah, the Jaredites being an important part of it. Their voyage to America became evidence of the fact, and we have their written history to sustain it, the book of Ether in the Book of Mormon.

# Chapter 3

# A PRAYER
# TO BE SPARED

The predicted scattering of the people to all parts of the world seemingly was known well in advance of the fact, since it appears to have been one reason for constructing the tower. The builders planned to erect both a city and a tower, "lest we be scattered abroad upon the face of the whole earth." (Genesis 11:4.)

Prophets may have warned them, since it was customary for the Lord to follow such a practice. But as Joseph Smith's revision indicates, "they hearkened not unto the Lord."

Notice of the confusion of tongues also was known previously at least to Jared and his brother, for they wished to avoid it.

Jared's brother was especially favored of the Lord because of his righteous life. In Ether we read:

"The brother of Jared being a large and mighty man, and a man highly favored of the Lord, Jared, his brother, said unto him: Cry unto the Lord, that he will not confound us that we may not understand our words.

"And it came to pass that the brother of Jared did cry unto the Lord, and the Lord had compassion upon Jared; therefore he did not confound the language of Jared; and Jared and his brother were not confounded."

But this did not satisfy Jared, who desired the same privilege for his friends. He appealed once more to his brother, saying, "Cry again unto the Lord, and it may be that he will turn away his anger from them who are our friends, that he confound not their language.

"And it came to pass that the brother of Jared did cry unto

the Lord, and the Lord had compassion upon their friends and their families also, that they were not confounded."

Jared still had further thoughts. He was concerned about the dispersion.

"And it came to pass that Jared spake again unto his brother, saying: Go and inquire of the Lord whether he will drive us out of the land, and if he will drive us out of the land, cry unto him whither we shall go. And who knoweth but the Lord will carry us forth into a land which is choice above all the earth? And if it so be, let us be faithful unto the Lord, that we may receive it for our inheritance.

"And it came to pass that the brother of Jared did cry unto the Lord according to that which had been spoken by the mouth of Jared.

"And it came to pass that the Lord did hear the brother of Jared, and had compassion upon him, and said unto him: Go to and gather together thy flocks, both male and female, of every kind; and also of the seed of the earth of every kind; and thy families; and also Jared thy brother and his family; and also thy friends and their families, and the friends of Jared and their families. And when thou hast done this thou shalt go at the head of them down into the valley which is northward. And there will I meet thee, and I will go before thee into a land which is choice above all the lands of the earth."

The Lord then made a great promise to these men, telling them, "There will I bless thee and thy seed, and raise up unto me of thy seed, and of the seed of thy brother, and they who shall go with thee, a great nation. And there shall be none greater than the nation which I will raise up unto me of thy seed, upon all the face of the earth. And thus I will do unto thee because this long time ye have cried unto me." (Ether 1:34-43.)

But like all other divine blessings, this, too, rested on the obedience of the people. Here was their opportunity. How would the Jaredites respond?

Centuries later the Lord made a similar prediction to the Twelve Tribes of Israel as Moses brought them back from

Egypt: "And it shall come to pass, if thou shalt hearken diligently unto the voice of the Lord thy God, to observe and to do all his commandments which I command thee this day, that the Lord thy God will set thee on high above all nations of the earth." (Deuteronomy 28:1.)

In Moses' day, Palestine was a promised land; it still is. The Lord placed conditions on its occupancy, however. He said to ancient Israel:

"Thou shalt therefore keep the commandments, and the statutes, and the judgments, which I command thee this day, to do them. Wherefore it shall come to pass, if ye hearken to these judgments, and keep, and do them, that the Lord thy God shall keep unto thee the covenant and the mercy which he sware unto thy fathers. . . . Thou shalt be blessed above all people." (Deuteronomy 7:11-14.)

To further impress this great lesson upon Israel, the Lord declared: "Behold, I set before you this day a blessing and a curse; a blessing, if ye obey the commandments of the Lord your God, which I command you this day: and a curse, if ye will not obey the commandments of the Lord your God, but turn aside out of the way which I command you this day, to go after other gods, which ye have not known." (Deuteronomy 11:26-28.)

Thus we see that the Lord desires his people to advance and prosper in the earth.

He promised the Jaredites they could become the world's greatest nation of that time. He promised Israel the same blessing for their day. And he offers great opportunities to us who live today in the choice land of America. (See Ether 2:9-12.)

But fulfillment of all of God's promises rests upon obedience to his laws. What will be the outcome for us? The Jaredites failed to reach their potential; so did the Twelve Tribes, and for the same reason. Will we profit by their examples?

# Chapter 4

# THE JAREDITES PLAN TO LEAVE

The Jaredites' journey to the Promised Land over both land and sea would be a long and tedious undertaking. The sea voyage alone was to last 344 days.

Jared made preparations very much as did Noah, for he was to bring with him some farm animals, seeds of various kinds, birds, and even swarms of bees. The bees were known as "deseret" (Ether 2:3), a name that has become familiar in western America. Live fish were included, too, being carried in a tank specially prepared for the purpose.

The journey was divided into two stages. The first part took the people to the seashore, where they awaited further instructions from the Lord, who would tell them how to cross the ocean.

"And it came to pass that when they had come down into the valley of Nimrod the Lord came down and talked with the brother of Jared; and he was in a cloud, and the brother of Jared saw him not.

"And it came to pass that the Lord commanded them that they should go forth into the wilderness, yea, into that quarter where there never had man been. And it came to pass that the Lord did go before them, and did talk with them as he stood in a cloud, and gave directions whither they should travel."

The journey to the sea coast was described in this way: "It came to pass that they did cross many waters, being directed continually by the hand of the Lord."

Again the Lord impressed upon them that the land to which he was taking them was indeed choice above all others. He "would not suffer that they should stop beyond the sea in the wilderness, but he would that they should come forth even unto the land of promise, which was choice above all other lands, which the Lord God had preserved for a righteous people."

Apparently in traveling to the coast the people had to cross other waters as well as land, and to do so they had to build barges. This gave them experience for later on, when they would build eight barges for the journey over the seas.

The Lord now said:

"Go to work and build, after the manner of barges which ye have hitherto built. And it came to pass that the brother of Jared did go to work, and also his brethren, and built barges after the manner which they had built, according to the instructions of the Lord. And they were small, and they were light upon the water, even like unto the lightness of a fowl upon the water.

"And they were built after a manner that they were exceedingly tight, even that they would hold water like unto a dish; and the bottom thereof was tight like unto a dish; and the sides thereof were tight like unto a dish; and the ends thereof were peaked; and the top thereof was tight like unto a dish; and the length thereof was the length of a tree; and the door thereof, when it was shut, was tight like unto a dish."

When the work was finished, the brother of Jared cried out: "O Lord, I have performed the work which thou hast commanded me, and I have made the barges according as thou hast directed me. And behold, O Lord, in them there is no light; whither shall we steer? And also we shall perish, for in them we cannot breathe, save it is the air which is in them; therefore we shall perish."

The Lord replied, "Behold, thou shalt make a hole in the top, and also in the bottom; and when thou shalt suffer for air thou shalt unstop the hole and receive air. And if it be so that the water come in upon thee, behold, ye shall stop the hole, that ye may not perish in the flood.

"And it came to pass that the brother of Jared did so, according as the Lord had commanded."

Ventilation was now provided, but there was yet the problem of light within the barges. The brother of Jared called on the

Lord again: "O Lord, behold I have done even as thou hast commanded me; and I have prepared the vessels for my people, and behold there is no light in them. Behold, O Lord, wilt thou suffer that we shall cross this great water in darkness?

"And the Lord said unto the brother of Jared: What will ye that I should do that ye may have light in your vessels? For behold, ye cannot have windows, for they will be dashed in pieces; neither shall ye take fire with you, for ye shall not go by the light of fire.

"For behold, ye shall be as a whale in the midst of the sea; for the mountain waves shall dash upon you. Nevertheless, I will bring you up again out of the depths of the sea; for the winds have gone forth out of my mouth, and also the rains and the floods have I sent forth.

"And behold, I prepare you against these things; for ye cannot cross this great deep save I prepare you against the waves of the sea, and the winds which have gone forth, and the floods which shall come. Therefore what will ye that I should prepare for you that ye may have light when ye are swallowed up in the depths of the sea?" (Ether 2.)

When the Lord asked, "What will ye that I should do that ye may have light in your vessels," he obviously expected the brother of Jared to exercise some ingenuity on his own part. The Lord would then expand his efforts as need be.

# Chapter 5

# THE LORD APPEARS

The brother of Jared went to a mountain called Shelem, where he cut out sixteen small stones that were white and clear. His plan was to ask the Lord to make them become self-luminous. He would put one in each end of every barge to provide light.

He carried the stones to the top of Mt. Shelem and there again approached the Lord:

"O Lord, thou hast said that we must be encompassed about by the floods. Now behold, O Lord, and do not be angry with thy servant because of his weakness before thee; for we know that thou art holy and dwellest in the heavens, and that we are unworthy before thee; because of the fall our natures have become evil continually; nevertheless, O Lord, thou hast given us a commandment that we must call upon thee, that from thee we may receive according to our desires.

"Behold, O Lord, thou hast smitten us because of our iniquity, and hast driven us forth, and for these many years we have been in the wilderness; nevertheless, thou hast been merciful unto us. O Lord, look upon me in pity, and turn away thine anger from this thy people, and suffer not that they shall go forth across this raging deep in darkness; but behold these things which I have molten out of the rock.

"And I know, O Lord, that thou hast all power, and can do whatsoever thou wilt for the benefit of man; therefore touch these stones, O Lord, with thy finger, and prepare them that they may shine forth in darkness; and they shall shine forth unto us in the vessels which we have prepared, that we may have light while we shall cross the sea.

"Behold, O Lord, thou canst do this. We know that thou art

able to show forth great power, which looks small unto the understanding of men."

Now came a miraculous answer to his prayer.

"And it came to pass that when the brother of Jared had said these words, behold, the Lord stretched forth his hand and touched the stones one by one with his finger. And the veil was taken from off the eyes of the brother of Jared, and he saw the finger of the Lord; and it was as the finger of a man, like unto flesh and blood; and the brother of Jared fell down before the Lord, for he was struck with fear.

"And the Lord saw that the brother of Jared had fallen to the earth; and the Lord said unto him: Arise, why hast thou fallen?

"And he saith unto the Lord: I saw the finger of the Lord, and I feared lest he should smite me; for I knew not that the Lord had flesh and blood.

"And the Lord said unto him: Because of thy faith thou hast seen that I shall take upon me flesh and blood; and never has man come before me with such exceeding faith as thou hast; for were it not so ye could not have seen my finger. Sawest thou more than this?

"And he answered: Nay; Lord, show thyself unto me.

"And the Lord said unto him: Believest thou the words which I shall speak?

"And he answered: Yea, Lord, I know that thou speakest the truth, for thou art a God of truth, and canst not lie.

"And when he had said these words, behold, the Lord showed himself unto him, and said: Because thou knowest these things ye are redeemed from the fall; therefore ye are brought back into my presence; therefore I show myself unto you. Behold, I am he who was prepared from the foundation of the world to redeem my people. Behold, I am Jesus Christ. I am the Father and the Son. In me shall all mankind have life, and that eternally, even they who shall believe on my name; and they shall become my sons and my daughters.

"And never have I showed myself unto man whom I have created, for never has man believed in me as thou hast. Seest thou that ye are created after mine own image? Yea, even all men were created in the beginning after mine own image. Behold, this body, which ye now behold, is the body of my spirit; and man have I created after the body of my spirit; and even as I appear unto thee to be in the spirit will I appear unto my people in the flesh."

This marvelous manifestation was recorded by the prophet Ether on the twenty-four gold plates found by the people of Limhi.

Moroni, who summarized Ether's work, including the account of the Savior's appearance to the brother of Jared, commented:

"And now, as I, Moroni, said I could not make a full account of these things which are written, therefore it sufficeth me to say that Jesus showed himself unto this man in the spirit, even after the manner and in the likeness of the same body even as he showed himself unto the Nephites.

"And he ministered unto him even as he ministered unto the Nephites; and all this, that this man might know that he was God, because of the many great works which the Lord had showed unto him.

"And because of the knowledge of this man he could not be kept from beholding within the veil; and he saw the finger of Jesus, which, when he saw, he fell with fear; for he knew that it was the finger of the Lord; and he had faith no longer, for he knew, nothing doubting.

"Wherefore, having this perfect knowledge of God, he could not be kept from within the veil; therefore he saw Jesus; and he did minister unto him.

"And it came to pass that the Lord said unto the brother of Jared: Behold, thou shalt not suffer these things which ye have seen and heard to go forth unto the world, until the time cometh that I shall glorify my name in the flesh; wherefore, ye shall treasure up the things which ye have seen and heard, and show it to no man.

"And behold, when ye shall come unto me, ye shall write

them and shall seal them up, that no one can interpret them; for ye shall write them in a language that they cannot be read.

"And behold, these two stones will I give unto thee, and ye shall seal them up also with the things which ye shall write. For behold, the language which ye shall write I have confounded; wherefore I will cause in my own due time that these stones shall magnify to the eyes of men these things which ye shall write."

The Lord revealed still further knowledge to the brother of Jared. He now gave him a vision in which he saw "all the inhabitants of the earth which had been, and also all that would be; and he withheld them not from his sight, even unto the ends of the earth.

"For he had said unto him in times before, that if he would believe in him that he could show unto him all things—it should be shown unto him; therefore the Lord could not withhold anything from him, for he knew that the Lord could show him all things."

The Lord then declared: "Write these things and seal them up; and I will show them in mine own due time unto the children of men.

"And it came to pass that the Lord commanded him that he should seal up the two stones which he had received, and show them not, until the Lord should show them unto the children of men." (Jared 3.)

As the Jaredites neared the time of their departure, they had to be taught one more lesson. The Promised Land to which they were going was sacred to the Lord, and he decreed that any people who lived there must serve him or be swept off. It was a clear warning and a demand for righteous living. Sin would nullify their right to be there.

# Chapter 6

# ABOVE ALL
# OTHER LANDS

Our earth is one of the most important planets in the universe and is close to the dearest interests of God. He created it for his own divine purpose, which is, to bring about our immortality and eternal life. (Moses 1:33, 39.) And he made it for his Only Begotten Son, our Savior, for whom it will be a dwelling place on reaching its celestial state.

The earth's destiny is to become like the orb where God dwells. When it is sanctified to be part of the celestial kingdom, it will serve as a Urim and Thummim to the people who dwell upon it. (See D&C 130:8-9.)

Although classed among the small globes in the galaxies, earth is one of the most significant. Jesus came here for his mortal life. No other orb in all creation was so honored. Here he accomplished his atonement, the most important event that has ever happened. Here also he overcame death and brought about the resurrection of all mankind.

In its celestialized form, this earth will become the home of the "church of the Firstborn," of Saints who have earned the highest glory in the mansions of God, to dwell there with Christ in eternity, for it will be his. (See D&C 76:54-70, 94; 130:8-9.)

Just as earth has special significance in the universe, so upon its surface is a particular geographic region of tremendous consequence, a place that is choice above all other parts of the world. It is a consecrated region reserved by the Almighty as the location on which he will bring about most of the greatest events of latter days and where already he has miraculously revealed his hand.

The selection and designation of this choice place came with Creation itself. Here the Lord planted a garden "eastward in Eden" where human life had its beginning. Here was the valley of Adam-ondi-Ahman, the sanctified gathering place. Here the Lord swept away the people of Noah because they polluted his holy land.

After the flood this region continued to be the choicest area on earth. Its status was not altered by the great deluge. "After the waters had receded from off the face of this land it became a choice land above all other lands, a chosen land of the Lord; wherefore the Lord would have that all men should serve him who dwell upon the face thereof."

So this most choice area had not lost its identity nor its destiny.

On this promised land the Savior ministered and established his church following his resurrection in Palestine. On this promised land he restored his church in latter days preparatory to his second coming. Here will be the location of the New Jerusalem, which will come down from heaven, a holy sanctuary of the Lord.

The earthly New Jerusalem will be built on this continent "unto a remnant of the seed of Joseph. . . . For as Joseph brought his father down into the land of Egypt, even so he died there; wherefore, the Lord brought a remnant of the seed of Joseph out of the land of Jerusalem, that he might be merciful unto the seed of Joseph that they should perish not, even as he was merciful unto the father of Joseph that he should perish not.

"Wherefore, the remnant of the house of Joseph shall be built upon this land; and it shall be a land of their inheritance; and they shall build up a holy city unto the Lord, like unto the Jerusalem of old; and they shall no more be confounded, until the end come when the earth shall pass away.

"And there shall be a new heaven and a new earth; and they shall be like unto the old save the old have passed away, and all things have become new.

"And then cometh the New Jerusalem; and blessed are they who dwell therein, for it is they whose garments are white through the blood of the Lamb; and they are they who are numbered among the remnant of the seed of Joseph, who were of the house of Israel.

"And then also cometh the Jerusalem of old; and the inhabitants thereof, blessed are they, for they have been washed in the blood of the Lamb; and they are they who were scattered and gathered in from the four quarters of the earth, and from the north countries, and are partakers of the fulfilling of the covenant which God made with their father, Abraham." (Ether 13: 2-11.)

In preparation for these great events, it was necessary that a remnant of the tribe of Joseph be brought here in advance. Thus, the Lord led Lehi and his party to this promised land, and Lehi blessed it for his family.

"Behold, said he, I have seen a vision, in which I know that Jerusalem is destroyed; and had we remained in Jerusalem we should also have perished.

"But, said he, notwithstanding our afflictions, we have obtained a land of promise, a land which is choice above all other lands; a land which the Lord God hath covenanted with me should be a land for the inheritance of my seed. Yea, the Lord hath covenanted this land unto me, and to my children forever, and also all those who should be led out of other countries by the hand of the Lord.

"Wherefore, I, Lehi, prophesy according to the workings of the Spirit which is in me, that there shall none come into this land save they shall be brought by the hand of the Lord.

"Wherefore, this land is consecrated unto him whom he shall bring. And if it so be that they shall serve him according to the commandments which he hath given, it shall be a land of liberty unto them; wherefore, they shall never be brought down into captivity; if so, it shall be because of iniquity; for if iniquity shall abound cursed shall be the land for their sakes, but unto the righteous it shall be blessed forever.

"And behold, it is wisdom that this land should be kept as

yet from the knowledge of other nations; for behold, many nations would overrun the land, that there would be no place for an inheritance.

"Wherefore, I, Lehi, have obtained a promise, that inasmuch as those whom the Lord God shall bring out of the land of Jerusalem shall keep his commandments, they shall prosper upon the face of this land; and they shall be kept from all other nations, that they may possess this land unto themselves. And if it so be that they shall keep his commandments they shall be blessed upon the face of this land, and there shall be none to molest them, nor to take away the land of their inheritance; and they shall dwell safely forever." (2 Nephi 1:4-9.)

Also in preparation for the great events of latter days, the Lord raised up "a mighty nation of the Gentiles" upon this land as a major step in opening the way for the worldwide preaching of the gospel before the end shall come. The establishment of this nation was seen in vision by Nephi (1 Nephi 13) and was predicted by the Savior himself.

"It is wisdom in the Father that they should be established in this land, and be set up as a free people by the power of the Father, that these things might come forth from them unto a remnant of your seed, that the covenant of the Father may be fulfilled which he hath covenanted with his people, O house of Israel." (3 Nephi 21:4.)

In the wisdom of our Heavenly Father, this great Gentile nation was to be brought into being and by his divine decree it must be free—free from domination by any other power, free from monarchs and dictators, having a form of government certain to provide the liberty under which his purposes could be achieved.

These events—all of them—were to be accomplished in this one selected region of the world, this most choice of all lands, America!

Understanding these facts is essential to our knowing why there is a Promised Land.

Since both a free government and a righteous people on

whom the Lord could depend are necessary to his planned use of this land, he laid down rules of conduct for whatever people came here to live.

"He had sworn in his wrath unto the brother of Jared, that whoso should possess this land of promise, from that time henceforth and forever, should serve him, the true and only God, or they should be swept off when the fulness of his wrath should come upon them.

"And now, we can behold the decrees of God concerning this land, that it is a land of promise; and whatsoever nation shall possess it shall serve God, or they shall be swept off when the fulness of his wrath shall come upon them. And the fulness of his wrath cometh upon them when they are ripened in iniquity.

"For behold, this is a land which is choice above all other lands; wherefore he that doth possess it shall serve God or shall be swept off; for it is the everlasting decree of God. And it is not until the fulness of iniquity among the children of the land, that they are swept off."

But these rules were not for ancient people alone. They apply to the great nation of the Gentiles just as well.

"And this cometh unto you, O ye Gentiles, that ye may know the decrees of God—that ye may repent, and not continue in your iniquities until the fulness come, that ye may not bring down the fulness of the wrath of God upon you as the inhabitants of the land have hitherto done.

"Behold, this is a choice land, and whatsoever nation shall possess it shall be free from bondage, and from captivity, and from all other nations under heaven, if they will but serve the God of the land, who is Jesus Christ, who hath been manifested by the things which we have written." (Ether 2:8-12.)

The conditions pertaining to the occupancy of America were stated plainly to the Nephites when they came here to live. (See 2 Nephi 1:4-9.)

The prophet Jacob spoke of the residence of the Gentiles on this land, declaring:

"This land, said God, shall be a land of thine inheritance, and the Gentiles shall be blessed upon the land. And this land shall be a land of liberty unto the Gentiles, and there shall be no kings upon the land, who shall raise up unto the Gentiles. And I will fortify this land against all other nations.

"And he that fighteth against Zion shall perish, saith God. For he that raiseth up a king against me shall perish, for I, the Lord, the king of heaven, will be their king, and I will be a light unto them forever, that hear my words.

"Wherefore, for this cause, that my covenants may be fulfilled which I have made unto the children of men, that I will do unto them while they are in the flesh, I must needs destroy the secret works of darkness, and of murders, and of abominations.

"Wherefore, he that fighteth against Zion, both Jew and Gentile, both bond and free, both male and female, shall perish; for they are they who are the whore of all the earth; for they who are not for me are against me, saith our God. For I will fulfil my promises which I have made unto the children of men, that I will do unto them while they are in the flesh."

The Lord then added this: "Wherefore, I will consecrate this land unto thy seed, and them who shall be numbered among thy seed, forever, for the land of their inheritance; for it is a choice land, saith God unto me, above all other lands, wherefore I will have all men that dwell thereon that they shall worship me, saith God." (2 Nephi 10:10-19.)

America is that choice and promised land. God will not permit any condition to prevent the fulfillment of divine prophecy. His plans for the Promised Land will neither change nor fail.

When the Jaredites ignored the rules of residency here, they were removed. The same was true of the Nephites. It happened to the people of Noah's day. Now, through the restoration of the gospel, comes our opportunity. But we are not to fail. The Lord expects that high degree of devotion from us that will assure our success. We must profit by the lessons of the past. His pattern will not change with respect to America. We must adjust our lives to his plans. With or without any of us, either as individuals or as groups, he will shape the events of these last days so that when he is ready, Zion will be established, and he will reign from this same promised land for a thousand years of Millennium. It will be from the headquarters he will establish here.

Then truly "out of Zion shall go forth the law, and the word of the Lord from Jerusalem. And he shall judge among the nations, and shall rebuke many people: and they shall beat their swords into plowshares, and their spears into pruninghooks: nation shall not lift up sword against nation, neither shall they learn war any more." (Isaiah 2:3-4.)

Hence it is that he calls and says, "O house of Jacob, come ye, and let us walk in the light of the Lord." (Isaiah 2:5.)

And hence it is that he requires obedience and righteous living on the part of his people, his chosen people on this his chosen land, for his own announced purpose.

# Chapter 7

# THE VOYAGE BEGINS

In many respects the voyage of the Jaredites to America resembled the experience of Noah in the ark. Each voyage lasted about a year. In each case, the people had to build their own ships. Animals and birds were involved, together with all the problems of providing for their care over many months.

As only a miracle made Noah's accomplishment possible, so it was with the Jaredites. The Lord gave similar attention to both. He had his own special purposes in each undertaking, and he assured their certain success.

The brother of Jared brought his luminous stones down from the mountain and placed one in each end of all eight barges. Then there was light.

"And it came to pass that when they had prepared all manner of food, that thereby they might subsist upon the water, and also food for their flocks and herds, and whatsoever beast or animal or fowl that they should carry with them—and it came to pass that when they had done all these things they got aboard of their vessels or barges, and set forth into the sea, commending themselves unto the Lord their God." (Ether 6:4.)

It is not certain how many people actually made this journey. The record says that Jared had four sons. The brother of Jared had both sons and daughters, but the number is not mentioned. "And the friends of Jared and his brother were in number about twenty and two souls; and they also begat sons and daughters before they came to the promised land." (Ether 6:16.) So no definite number was mentioned.

The ships apparently were somewhat like submarines, for they could travel both on the surface of the sea and beneath it.

They were not self-propelled, but were totally dependent on divine power to make the journey.

The Lord "caused that there should be a furious wind blow upon the face of the waters, towards the promised land; and thus they were tossed upon the waves of the sea before the wind.

"And it came to pass that they were many times buried in the depths of the sea, because of the mountain waves which broke upon them, and also the great and terrible tempests which were caused by the fierceness of the wind.

"And it came to pass that when they were buried in the deep there was no water that could hurt them, their vessels being tight like unto a dish, and also they were tight like unto the ark of Noah; therefore when they were encompassed about by many waters they did cry unto the Lord, and he did bring them forth again upon the top of the waters.

"And it came to pass that the wind did never cease to blow towards the promised land while they were upon the waters; and thus they were driven forth before the wind. . . . And no monster of the sea could break them, neither whale that could mar them; and they did have light continually, whether it was above the water or under the water."

Knowing that they must rely entirely on the Lord, not only to reach the Promised Land but also to preserve their lives, the people were humble and devoted. "They did sing praises unto the Lord; yea, the brother of Jared did sing praises unto the Lord, and he did thank and praise the Lord all the day long; and when the night came, they did not cease to praise the Lord."

The sea voyage lasted for 344 days, and at last they landed on the shore of the promised land. "When they had set their feet upon the shores of the promised land they bowed themselves down upon the face of the land, and did humble themselves before the Lord, and did shed tears of joy before the Lord, because of the multitude of his tender mercies over them."

Since they had brought seeds of various kinds as well as some animals, the people began to establish farms at once.

Sincerely grateful for their safe passage to America, they worshipped the Lord with great devotion, "and they were taught to walk humbly before the Lord." Since the brother of Jared had such a close relationship with God, it is not surprising that the record adds, "And they were also taught from on high. And it came to pass that they began to spread upon the face of the land, and to multiply and to till the earth; and they did wax strong in the land."

# Chapter 8

# THE FIRST JAREDITE KING

**M**ost ancient peoples were accustomed to being governed by kings.

Jared and his brother had provided leadership for their colony from the time they left the tower of Babel. They had been guided by continuous revelation and had therefore provided the group with inspired direction.

When the people saw that both Jared and his brother were nearing the end of their lives, they immediately desired a king to rule over them.

This deeply concerned the brother of Jared, who opposed them, saying, "Surely this thing leadeth into captivity." (Ether 6:23.) He feared the evils that wicked kings could bring upon the people, even as did Mosiah centuries later when he established a free government among the Nephites. (Mosiah 29:17.) It was Mosiah who had declared:

"Now it is better that a man should be judged of God than of man, for the judgments of God are always just, but the judgments of man are not always just.

"Therefore, if it were possible that you could have just men to be your kings, who would establish the laws of God, and judge this people according to his commandments, yea, if ye could have men for your kings who would do even as my father Benjamin did for this people—I say unto you, if this could always be the case then it would be expedient that ye should always have kings to rule over you. . . .

"Now I say unto you, that because all men are not just it is not expedient that ye should have a king or kings to rule over you. For behold, how much iniquity doth one wicked king cause to be committed, yea, and what great destruction! . . .

"And behold, now I say unto you, ye cannot dethrone an iniquitous king save it be through much contention, and the shedding of much blood. For behold, he has his friends in iniquity, and he keepeth his guards about him; and he teareth up the laws of those who have reigned in righteousness before him; and he trampleth under his feet the commandments of God; and he enacteth laws, and sendeth them forth among his people, yea, laws after the manner of his own wickedness; and whosoever doth not obey his laws he causeth to be destroyed; and whosoever doth rebel against him he will send his armies against them to war, and if he can he will destroy them; and thus an unrighteous king doth pervert the ways of all righteousness.

"And now behold I say unto you, it is not expedient that such abominations should come upon you. Therefore, choose you by the voice of this people, judges, that ye may be judged according to the laws which have been given you by our fathers, which are correct, and which were given them by the hand of the Lord.

"Now it is not common that the voice of the people desireth anything contrary to that which is right; but it is common for the lesser part of the people to desire that which is not right; therefore this shall ye observe and make it your law—to do your business by the voice of the people.

"And if the time comes that the voice of the people doth choose iniquity, then is the time that the judgments of God will come upon you; yea, then is the time he will visit you with great destruction even as he has hitherto visited this land." (Mosiah 29:12-13, 16-17, 21-27.)

Mosiah told the Nephites that this promised land should be free. "The sins of many people have been caused by the iniquities of their kings," he said; "therefore their iniquities are answered upon the heads of their kings. And now I desire that this inequality should be no more in this land, especially among this my people; but I desire that this land be a land of liberty, and every man may enjoy his rights and privileges alike, so long as the Lord sees fit that we may live and inherit the land, yea, even as long as any of our posterity remains upon the face of the land." (Mosiah 29:31-32.)

This was a great lesson in the interdependence of righteousness and freedom. Mosiah was a prophet of the Lord, and he spoke with authority.

The brother of Jared was inspired by that same power. He could foresee evil in the establishment of a kingdom among the Jaredites, and so he urged against it. He had been present when the Lord laid down rules for the occupancy of the Promised Land, and he had no desire to avoid them.

The Lord had been explicit in defining his terms. He swore in his wrath "unto the brother of Jared, that whoso should possess this land of promise, from that time henceforth and forever, should serve him, the true and only God, or they should be swept off when the fulness of his wrath should come upon them.

"And now, we can behold the decrees of God concerning this land, that it is a land of promise; and whatsoever nation shall possess it shall serve God, or they shall be swept off when the fulness of his wrath shall come upon them. And the fulness of his wrath cometh upon them when they are ripened in iniquity.

"For behold, this is a land which is choice above all other lands; wherefore he that doth possess it shall serve God or shall be swept off; for it is the everlasting decree of God. And it is not until the fulness of iniquity among the children of the land, that they are swept off." (Ether 2:8-10.)

When the Lord had thus "sworn in his wrath" to the brother of Jared, could his words be easily forgotten?

So it was that Jared's brother opposed Jared and the others in asking for a king. "Surely this thing leadeth into captivity," he warned.

But Jared did not agree. He wished to yield to the desires of the people. He said to his brother, "Suffer them that they may have a king. . . . Choose ye out from among our sons a king, even whom ye will."

The people chose the firstborn of the brother of Jared,

whose name was Pagag. "And it came to pass that he refused and would not be their king. And the people would that his father should constrain him, but his father would not; and he commanded them that they should constrain no man to be their king.

"And it came to pass that they chose all the brothers of Pagag, and they would not.

"And it came to pass that neither would the sons of Jared, even all save it were one; and Orihah was anointed to be king over the people." (Ether 6:24-27.)

# Chapter 9

# THE FIRST
# JAREDITE WAR

**A**mbition to rule over others proved to be one of the fatal stumbling blocks of the rising new leaders of the Jaredites. The lust for power led to intrigue of every kind, even to murder, as sons dethroned their fathers, jealous fathers destroyed their own sons who might be heirs to the throne, and brothers took the lives of each other. Family feuds were common.

Though there were righteous and prosperous periods in the history of the Jaredites, wickedness was the dominating factor over a large part of their existence. The people ignored the decrees of the Lord despite constant reminders by prophets sent from time to time, until eventually the cup of their iniquity overflowed into their final destruction.

Inspired by the saintly example of the brother of Jared, the people at first did serve the Lord. Their gratitude for a safe voyage to America lingered with them, and they worshipped the mighty Being who had brought them there. So it was that the first king of the Jaredites was a righteous man.

When Orihah was anointed as the first king, "the people began to prosper; and they became exceedingly rich.

"And it came to pass that Jared died, and his brother also.

"And it came to pass that Orihah did walk humbly before the Lord, and did remember how great things the Lord had done for his father, and also taught his people how great things the Lord had done for their fathers." (Ether 6:28-30.)

The record says that Orihah "did execute judgment upon the land in righteousness all his days, whose days were exceedingly many. And he begat sons and daughters; yea, he begat thirty and one, among whom were twenty and three sons. And it came to pass that he also begat Kib in his old age. And it came to pass that Kib reigned in his stead; and Kib begat Corihor."

Corihor was a rebel. Gathering his friends about him, he moved away from the main colony and set up a community that he called Nehor. His sons and daughters "were exceedingly fair"; so attractive were they that people left the main colony to become members of Corihor's group. This dissension grew until Corihor "gathered together an army" with which he invaded the land Moron, where his father, the king, lived. He took Kib prisoner and kept him in captivity until the king became very old. In the meantime, Corihor crowned himself and ruled over the land.

In his old age, and while still a prisoner, Kib had a son named Shule, who "waxed strong, and became mighty as to the strength of a man; and he was also mighty in judgment." Shule was angry with Corihor for having kept their father, Kib, in lifelong captivity, so he decided to overthrow Corihor and restore the throne to Kib.

Shule went to a nearby mountain known as Ephraim, and there, according to the record, "he did molten out of the hill, and made swords out of steel for those whom he had drawn away with him; and after he had armed them with swords he returned to the city Nehor, and gave battle unto his brother Corihor, by which means he obtained the kingdom and restored it unto his father Kib."

In gratitude for his son's courage and loyalty, Kib now bestowed the kingdom upon Shule, and Shule "began to reign in the stead of his father. And it came to pass that he did execute judgment in righteousness; and he did spread his kingdom upon all the face of the land, for the people had become exceedingly numerous. And it came to pass that Shule also begat many sons and daughters."

The unusual thing now happened. Corihor repented, and such good relationships with the family were restored that Shule gave Corihor responsibilities in the government.

Corihor continued faithful, but he had a son named Noah,

who was as rebellious as his father had formerly been. Noah attacked King Shule, seized control over a portion of the kingdom, and captured the king, who was carried off to prison.

"It came to pass as he was about to put him to death, the sons of Shule crept into the house of Noah by night and slew him, and broke down the door of the prison and brought out their father, and placed him upon his throne in his own kingdom.

"Wherefore, the son of Noah did build up his kingdom in his stead; nevertheless they did not gain power any more over Shule the king, and the people who were under the reign of Shule the king did prosper exceedingly and wax great.

"And the country was divided; and there were two kingdoms, the kingdom of Shule, and the kingdom of Cohor, the son of Noah." (Ether 7:1-20.)

Experiences such as these became typical among the Jaredites, and from generation to generation throughout the history of the nation they were repeated frequently.

# Chapter 10

# PROPHETIC WARNINGS

**A**lready the Jaredites were slipping into the pattern that eventually destroyed them. God was forgotten. Greed and avarice characterized their lives, and some of them actually turned to idolatry. War was still with them. Although Noah had been assassinated, one of his sons, named Cohor, assumed his father's role.

Cohor was determined to kill Shule, take his throne, and unite the kingdom under himself. A new war began, and Cohor invaded the kingdom of Shule, but Shule defeated him, killing him.

Cohor had a son, Nimrod, who had opposed his father's ambitions. The son became ruler after Cohor and "gave up the kingdom of Cohor unto Shule, and he did gain favor in the eyes of Shule; wherefore Shule did bestow great favors upon him, and he did do in the kingdom of Shule according to his desires."

Because of the political rebellions and increasing wickedness of the people, the Lord again sent prophets to warn them, "prophesying that the wickedness and idolatry of the people was bringing a curse upon the land, and they should be destroyed if they did not repent."

The people mocked the prophets, reviled them, and persecuted them severely. Shule still tried to govern righteously and, seeing the persecution, "did execute judgment against all those who did revile against the prophets.

"He did execute a law throughout all the land, which gave power unto the prophets that they should go whithersoever they would; and by this cause the people were brought unto repentance. And because the people did repent of their iniquities and idolatries the Lord did spare them, and they began to prosper again in the land. And it came to pass that Shule begat sons and daughters in his old age."

Shule remembered the teachings of his fathers, including the miracle of their coming to the Promised Land, "wherefore he did execute judgment in righteousness all his days." (Ether 7:21-27.) But peace was short-lived. The ambition to rule seemed to be irrepressible.

One of the successors of Shule was Omer, whose son Jared rebelled against him, seeking the throne. (See Ether 8:1-3.)

As an example of the treason and corruption that constantly surrounded the throne, we have statements such as these:

"It came to pass that Hearthom reigned in the stead of his father. And when Hearthom had reigned twenty and four years, behold, the kingdom was taken away from him. And he served many years in captivity, yea, even all the remainder of his days.

"And he begat Heth, and Heth lived in captivity all his days. And Heth begat Aaron, and Aaron dwelt in captivity all his days; and he begat Amnigaddah, and Amnigaddah also dwelt in captivity all his days; and he begat Coriantum, and Coriantum dwelt in captivity all his days; and he begat Com.

"And it came to pass that Com drew away the half of the kingdom. And he reigned over the half of the kingdom forty and two years; and he went to battle against the king, Amgid, and they fought for the space of many years, during which time Com gained power over Amgid, and obtained power over the remainder of the kingdom.

"And in the days of Com there began to be robbers in the land; and they adopted the old plans, and administered oaths after the manner of the ancients, and sought again to destroy the kingdom.

"Now Com did fight against them much; nevertheless, he did not prevail against them." (Ether 10:30-34.)

It seems incredible that people who had had such a spiritual and miraculous beginning would sink to such depths.

# Chapter 11

# A SCHEMING
# PRINCESS

Lust feeds on lust, and it seems to have no bounds when it takes over the human mind.

When King Shule died, his son Omer came to the throne. He was a good man, but he was forced to spend half of his days as a prisoner of his son Jared, who "set his heart upon the kingdom and upon the glory of the world."

Jared, a flatterer, went among the people with cunning words, sowing dissension against his father. Soon half the kingdom followed him. Arming his men, he attacked the palace and took his father captive. The record says that Omer was "in captivity the half of his days." However, he had two loyal sons, Esrom and Coriantumr, who raised an army and attacked their brother Jared. In their night assault they killed all of Jared's guards and made ready to kill him, but he pleaded for his life and promised that, if spared, he would return the kingdom to his father, Omer. This was accomplished, but Jared never gave up his yearning for the throne.

Jared had a scheming daughter who hoped to recover the crown for her father. She devised a plan by which her grandfather, King Omer, would be assassinated, and her own father, Jared, returned to power.

"Now the daughter of Jared was exceedingly fair. And it came to pass that she did talk with her father, and said unto him: Whereby hath my father so much sorrow? Hath he not read the record which our fathers brought across the great deep? Behold, is there not an account concerning them of old, that they by their secret plans did obtain kingdoms and great glory?

"And now, therefore, let my father send for Akish, the son

of Kimnor; and behold, I am fair, and I will dance before him, and I will please him, that he will desire me to wife; wherefore if he shall desire of thee that ye shall give unto him me to wife, then shall ye say: I will give her if ye will bring unto me the head of my father, the king."

Jared sent for Akish, who accepted the invitation. The princess danced before him, and "she pleased him, insomuch that he desired her to wife. And it came to pass that he said unto Jared: Give her unto me to wife. And Jared said unto him: I will give her unto you, if ye will bring unto me the head of my father, the king."

Akish was willing.

"It came to pass that Akish gathered in unto the house of Jared all his kinsfolk, and said unto them: Will ye swear unto me that ye will be faithful unto me in the thing which I shall desire of you?

"And it came to pass that they all sware unto him, by the God of heaven, and also by the heavens, and also by the earth, and by their heads, that whoso should vary from the assistance which Akish desired should lose his head; and whoso should divulge whatsoever thing Akish made known unto them, the same should lose his life.

"And it came to pass that thus they did agree with Akish. And Akish did administer unto them the oaths which were given by them of old who also sought power, which had been handed down even from Cain, who was a murderer from the beginning. . . .

"And it was the daughter of Jared who put it into his heart to search up these things of old; and Jared put it into the heart of Akish; wherefore, Akish administered it unto his kindred and friends, leading them away by fair promises to do whatsoever thing he desired.

"And it came to pass that they formed a secret combination, even as they of old; which combination is most abominable and wicked above all, in the sight of God; for the Lord worketh not in secret combinations, neither doth he will that man should shed blood, but in all things hath forbidden it, from the beginning of man."

But the Lord intervened. He warned King Omer in a dream "that he should depart out of the land; wherefore Omer departed out of the land with his family, and traveled many days, and came over and passed by the hill of Shim, and came over by the place where the Nephites were destroyed, and from thence eastward, and came to a place which was called Ablom, by the seashore, and there he pitched his tent, and also his sons and his daughters, and all his household, save it were Jared and his family."

With his father gone, Jared was now anointed king. He prepared at once for the wedding of his daughter and Akish. This did not satisfy Akish. He wanted the throne for himself.

"It came to pass that Akish sought the life of his father-in-law; and he applied unto those whom he had sworn by the oath of the ancients, and they obtained the head of his father-in-law, as he sat upon his throne, giving audience to his people. For so great had been the spreading of this wicked and secret society that it had corrupted the hearts of all the people; therefore Jared was mudered upon his throne, and Akish reigned in his stead."

Akish had a son of whose ability he became very jealous. He cast the young man into prison, where he starved to death. This angered another son, whose name was Nimrah. He gathered his friends about him, and the entire group went over to King Omer, joining forces with him.

Akish had other sons, and they also opposed their father, but they had ambitions of their own. They brought about a rebellion by the use of bribery.

"Now the people of Akish were desirous for gain, even as Akish was desirous for power; wherefore, the sons of Akish did offer them money, by which means they drew away the more part of the people after them.

"And there began to be a war between the sons of Akish and

Akish, which lasted for the space of many years, yea, unto the destruction of nearly all the people of the kingdom, yea, even all, save it were thirty souls, and they who fled with the house of Omer.

"Wherefore, Omer was restored again to the land of his inheritance." (Ether 8; 9:1-13.)

Such was the intrigue and wickedness among the Jaredites.

# Chapter 12

# THE GOOD
# KING EMER

In his old age, King Omer had a son named Emer, whom he anointed king to succeed him.

"And after that he had anointed Emer to be king he saw peace in the land for the space of two years, and he died, having seen exceedingly many days, which were full of sorrow. And it came to pass that Emer did reign in his stead, and did fill the steps of his father."

The reign of Emer was a golden age for the Jaredites. In a matter of sixty-two years, the kingdom went from a state of conflict and corruption to one of peace and prosperity, all because the king taught the people to serve the Lord, and He responded in kind.

The Lord removed the curse from the land and permitted the people to become "exceedingly rich—having all manner of fruit, and of grain, and of silks, and of fine linen, and of gold, and of silver, and of precious things; and also all manner of cattle, of oxen, and cows, and of sheep, and of swine, and of goats, and also many other kinds of animals which were useful for the food of man.

"And they also had horses, and asses, and there were elephants and cureloms and cumoms; all of which were useful unto man, and more especially the elephants and cureloms and cumoms.

"And thus the Lord did pour out his blessings upon this land, which was choice above all other lands."

Once again the Lord reminded his people that they were living in a sacred land. "He commanded that whoso should possess the land should possess it unto the Lord, or they should be destroyed when they were ripened in iniquity; for upon such, saith the Lord: I will pour out the fulness of my wrath."

Throughout his days, Emer ruled in righteousness. He was so blessed of the Lord that "he even saw the Son of Righteousness, and did rejoice and glory in his day; and he died in peace."

Emer was succeeded by his son Coriantum, also a righteous man. In his day, Coriantum built "many mighty cities, and did administer that which was good unto his people in all his days." Coriantum lived to be 142 years old, and his wife lived to be 102. They had no children. However, Coriantum married again after his elderly wife died. His new wife, a young woman, gave him both sons and daughters, including Com, who became king after Coriantum. (Ether 9:14-25.)

# Chapter 13

# LIB'S RIGHTEOUS REIGN

**L**ib was one of the great kings of the Jaredites. Though he lived many generations after Emer and Coriantum, Lib's reign is another example of the heights the Jaredites could achieve when they lived righteously. The people grew and prospered greatly under his rule.

Lib arose out of a history of rebellion and captivity, but he did not submit to it himself. An ancestor named Kim, one of the Jaredite kings, lived most of his life in captivity, having been forced from the throne. His son Levi "did serve in captivity after the death of his father, for the space of forty and two years," but then obtained the kingdom for himself by overpowering the usurper.

Levi then did that which "was right in the sight of the Lord; and the people did prosper in the land; and he did live to a good old age, and begat sons and daughters; and he also begat Corom, whom he anointed king in his stead."

"And it came to pass that Corom did that which was good in the sight of the Lord all his days; and he begat many sons and daughters; and after he had seen many days he did pass away, even like unto the rest of the earth; and Kish reigned in his stead.

"And it came to pass that Kish passed away also, and Lib reigned in his stead."

Lib, a hunter, turned "the land southward" into a game preserve. "Wherefore they did go into the land southward, to hunt food for the people of the land, for the land was covered with animals of the forest. And Lib also himself became a great hunter.

"And they built a great city by the narrow neck of land, by the place where the sea divides the land. And they did preserve the land southward for a wilderness, to get game. And the whole face of the land northward was covered with inhabitants."

The entire nation prospered under Lib's rule, again illustrating the truth of the Lord's promise that if they would serve the God of the land, they would be prospered in that land.

"They were exceedingly industrious, and they did buy and sell and traffic one with another, that they might get gain.

"And they did work in all manner of ore, and they did make gold, and silver, and iron, and brass, and all manner of metals; and they did dig it out of the earth; wherefore they did cast up mighty heaps of earth to get ore, of gold, and of silver, and of iron, and of copper. And they did work all manner of fine work.

"And they did have silks, and fine-twined linen; and they did work all manner of cloth, that they might clothe themselves from their nakedness.

"And they did make all manner of tools to till the earth, both to plow and to sow, to reap and to hoe, and also to thrash. And they did make all manner of tools with which they did work their beasts. And they did make all manner of weapons of war. And they did work all manner of work of exceedingly curious workmanship.

"And never could be a people more blessed than were they, and more prospered by the hand of the Lord. And they were in a land that was choice above all lands, for the Lord had spoken it.

"And it came to pass that Lib did live many years, and begat sons and daughters; and he also begat Hearthom." (Ether 10: 13-29.)

# Chapter 14

# THEY RISE
# AND FALL

**N**ot all the strong kings among the Jaredites were good men. Some were righteous, of course, but many were warmongers and moral lepers.

Heth, one of the worst of them, fostered evil throughout the realm and killed the prophets when the Lord made attempts to call the people back to repentance.

Heth, who knew the ancient secret combinations, was a murderer. He gathered his friends about him and put them under oath to do his will regardless of what it might be, even to the taking of life in the royal family.

Heth's father, Com, son of Coriantum, had reigned for forty-nine years. Assisted by his secret followers, Heth now coveted the throne and planned to kill his father to obtain it. "And it came to pass that he did dethrone his father, for he slew him with his own sword; and he did reign in his stead."

Under Heth's regime, wickedness spread rapidly throughout the kingdom. Prophets came into the land again, "crying repentance unto them—that they must prepare the way of the Lord or there should come a curse upon the face of the land; yea, even there should be a great famine, in which they should be destroyed if they did not repent."

Neither the people nor the king believed what the prophets told them. Instead, they persecuted them, threw them into prison or into deep pits in the ground, and left them there to die. "They did all these things according to the commandment of the king, Heth," showing to what depths he had plunged.

Then came the famine, and many in the kingdom died of starvation, "for there was no rain upon the face of the earth."

The Lord sent a second curse upon them, an influx of

poisonous serpents that attacked the people and caused tremendous fear among them. The snakes also attacked the livestock, which began to flee "towards the land southward" to escape. When the livestock died from poisonous bites, the people ate their carcasses in an attempt to avoid starving from the famine. But the Lord sealed up the passage to the land southward by allowing the poisonous serpents to hedge up that way, and whoever tried to pass was attacked.

One who died in this famine was King Heth himself, "and all his household save it were Shez."

When the people saw how desperate was their situation from both famine and serpents, they began to remember what the prophets had said, and they turned again to the Lord.

"It came to pass that when they had humbled themselves sufficiently before the Lord he did send rain upon the face of the earth; and the people began to revive again, and there began to be fruit in the north countries, and in all the countries round about. And the Lord did show forth his power unto them in preserving them from famine."

Shez, son of Heth, now became king. Determined to serve the Lord, he "began to build up again a broken people. And it came to pass that Shez did remember the destruction of his fathers, and he did build up a righteous kingdom; for he remembered what the Lord had done in bringing Jared and his brother across the deep; and he did walk in the ways of the Lord; and he begat sons and daughters."

Shez had a son named Shez, who rose up against him, seizing the kingdom. But he was killed "by the hand of a robber, because of his exceeding riches." With his death, the rebellion ended, and the father regained the throne. "And it came to pass that his father did build up many cities upon the face of the land."

When Shez died, his next son, Riplakish, obtained the crown. This son was corrupt and gave affront to the Lord from the beginning of his reign. He had many wives and concubines and coveted wealth, which he spent in lavish living. He was cruel to his subjects, exacting heavy taxes and forcing labor from them.

Riplakish not only erected costly buildings but also many prisons, "and whoso would not be subject unto taxes he did cast into prison; and whoso was not able to pay taxes he did cast into prison; and he did cause that they should labor continually for their support; and whoso refused to labor he did cause to be put to death.

"Wherefore he did obtain all his fine work, yea, even his fine gold he did cause to be refined in prison; and all manner of fine workmanship he did cause to be wrought in prison. And it came to pass that he did afflict the people with his whoredoms and abominations."

In the uprising against the wicked rule of Riplakish, the king himself was killed, and his entire family was driven out of the land. (Ether 9:25–10:8.)

# Chapter 15

# OTHER
# REBELLIONS

**M**any years later a persuasive man named Morianton coveted the throne. A descendant of Riplakish, he organized a rebellion to seize the kingdom.

In that day there were many outcasts from among the main body of the people, people who were bitter against the ruling power. Morianton went among them, stirring them up to fight and organizing them into an army. When he felt they were strong enough, his forces attacked and gained power over many cities.

"The war became exceedingly sore, and did last for the space of many years." Finally Morianton "did gain power over all the land, and did establish himself king over all the land."

But Morianton was different from some of his predecessors. In order to gain favor with the people he had conquered, he immediately lowered their taxes and reduced other demands upon them. This pleased his subjects, and they willingly crowned him king.

The record says that although Morianton seemed to "do justice " to the people, he did not do so "unto himself because of his many whoredoms; wherefore he was cut off from the presence of the Lord.

"And it came to pass that Morianton built up many cities, and the people became exceedingly rich under his reign, both in buildings, and in gold and silver, and in raising grain, and in flocks, and herds, and such things which had been restored unto them. And Morianton did live to an exceedingly great age." (Ether 10:9-12.) He it was who begat Kim, the first of a line of captive kings and great-great-grandfather of Lib, the righteous king.

In spite of Lib's reign in which the people served the Lord, the Jaredites had established for themselves a pattern of captivity and rebellion. Hearthom, the son of Lib, was brought into captivity, and four generations of his descendants were kept captive. Not until the rebellion of Com was the kingdom restored to the line of Hearthom, and for a period the Jaredites had another righteous king.

War followed swiftly, though, as Com's sons, Shiblom and his brother, fought each other. Conditions were terrible: "There began to be wars and contentions in all the land, and also many famines and pestilences, insomuch that there was a great destruction, such an one as never had been known upon the face of the earth; and all this came to pass in the days of Shiblom."

Shiblom was finally slain, and Seth, the son of Shiblom, was imprisoned. Ahah, the son of Seth, regained the kingdom, but he and his son Ethem, the next king, were extremely wicked rulers.

In the days of King Ethem, the Lord sent many prophets again among the people. "Yea, they did prophesy that the Lord would utterly destroy them from off the face of the earth except they repented of their iniquities."

However, the people "hardened their hearts, and would not hearken" to the words of the prophets. "And the prophets mourned and withdrew from among the people."

Ethem's successor was his son Moron, who also was a wicked man.

"It came to pass that there arose a rebellion among the people, because of that secret combination which was built up to get power and gain; and there arose a mighty man among them in iniquity, and gave battle unto Moron, in which he did overthrow the half of the kingdom; and he did maintain the half of the kingdom for many years. And it came to pass that Moron did overthrow him, and did obtain the kingdom again.

"And it came to pass that there arose another mighty man; and he was a descendant of the brother of Jared. And it came to pass that he did overthrow Moron and obtain the kingdom;

wherefore, Moron dwelt in captivity all the remainder of his days; and he begat Coriantor. And it came to pass that Coriantor dwelt in captivity all his days.

"And in the days of Coriantor there also came many prophets, and prophesied of great and marvelous things, and cried repentance unto the people, and except they should repent the Lord God would execute judgment against them to their utter destruction; and that the Lord God would send or bring forth another people to possess the land, by his power, after the manner by which he brought their fathers.

"And they did reject all the words of the prophets, because of their secret society and wicked abominations." (Ether 11.)

And so the nation went from one kind of iniquity to another, establishing the pattern for their final destruction. They became like the Nephites after them, a tragic example of the fruits of disobedience.

# Chapter 16

# THE PROPHET ETHER

The days of the Jaredites were fast coming to a close when the Lord raised up Ether, the last of their prophets.

The son of King Coriantor, Ether was apparently born while his father was a prisoner, for the record says he "dwelt in captivity all his days." His grandfather, King Moron, had been overthrown by a usurper "and dwelt in captivity all the remainder of his days." (Ether 11:17-19.) It was one more in a long series of similar episodes where it seemed no ruler was secure on his throne.

Ether started his ministry during Coriantumr's reign, when he "began to prophesy unto the people, for he could not be restrained because of the Spirit of the Lord which was in him. For he did cry from the morning, even until the going down of the sun, exhorting the people to believe in God unto repentance lest they should be destroyed, saying unto them that by faith all things are fulfilled."

Ether warned the people to repent lest destruction should come upon them, but he also preached of a better world, a happier life to be obtained by faith in God. Wherefore, he said, "whoso believeth in God might with surety hope for a better world, yea, even a place at the right hand of God, which hope cometh of faith, maketh an anchor to the souls of men, which would make them sure and steadfast, always abounding in good works, being led to glorify God.

"And it came to pass that Ether did prophesy great and marvelous things unto the people, which they did not believe, because they saw them not."

The people's unbelief did not deter Ether. Filled with the spirit of revelation, he told them of the greatness of the Promised Land and the blessings that were yet to come upon it. He described the coming of Lehi's family, which would be a remnant of the tribe of Joseph who was sold into Egypt, and explained that this land would be an inheritance for them.

Ether spoke of the New Jerusalem to come in the last days, and of the new heaven and new earth mentioned in prophecy, adding, "and they shall be like unto the old save the old have passed away, and all things have become new."

He spoke of those who would live in the New Jerusalem: "Blessed are they, for they have been washed in the blood of the Lamb; and they are they who were scattered and gathered in from the four quarters of the earth, and from the north countries, and are partakers of the fulfilling of the covenant which God made with their father, Abraham. And when these things come, bringeth to pass the scripture which saith, there are they who were first, who shall be last; and there are they who were last, who shall be first."

But this was all wasted on the wicked Jaredites, who cast Ether out of their midst. Therefore, "he hid himself in the cavity of a rock by day, and by night he went forth viewing the things which should come upon the people. And as he dwelt in the cavity of the rock he made the remainder of this record, viewing the destructions which came upon the people, by night."

A great war broke out in the same year that Ether was rejected by the people, as secret combinations of men planned to overthrow King Coriantumr. The scripture says: "Now Coriantumr, having studied, himself, in all the arts of war and all the cunning of the world, wherefore he gave battle unto them who sought to destroy him.

"But he repented not, neither his fair sons nor daughters; neither the fair sons and daughters of Cohor; neither the fair sons and daughters of Corihor; and in fine, there were none of the fair sons and daughters upon the face of the whole earth who repented of their sins.

"Wherefore, it came to pass that in the first year that Ether dwelt in the cavity of a rock, there were many people who were slain by the sword of those secret combinations, fighting against Coriantumr that they might obtain the kingdom."

In the second year of this war, the Lord directed Ether to "go and prophesy unto Coriantumr that, if he would repent, and all his household, the Lord would give unto him his kingdom and spare the people—

"Otherwise they should be destroyed, and all his household save it were himself. And he should only live to see the fulfilling of the prophecies which had been spoken concerning another people receiving the land for their inheritance; and Coriantumr should receive a burial by them; and every soul should be destroyed save it were Coriantumr."

But the king would not listen. "It came to pass that Coriantumr repented not, neither his household, neither the people; and the wars ceased not; and they sought to kill Ether, but he fled from before them and hid again in the cavity of the rock."

Further uprisings occurred and heavy losses resulted from the conflicts. One aggressor, Shared by name, attacked Coriantumr in battle and dethroned him. After four years, Coriantumr's sons defeated Shared and restored their father to the throne. But Shared returned to fight against Coriantumr in a battle that lasted three days.

"It came to pass that Coriantumr beat [Shared], and did pursue him until he came to the plains of Heshlon. And it came to pass that Shared gave him battle again upon the plains; and behold, he did beat Coriantumr, and drove him back again to the valley of Gilgal. And Coriantumr gave Shared battle again in the valley of Gilgal, in which he beat Shared and slew him. And Shared wounded Coriantumr in his thigh, that he did not go to battle again for the space of two years, in which time all the people upon the face of the land were shedding blood, and there was none to restrain them."

During this same period, an epidemic of crime developed among the Jaredites. The record says, "There were robbers, and in fine, all manner of wickedness upon all the face of the land."

A great curse came upon the land "because of the iniquity of the people, in which, if a man should lay his tool or his sword upon his shelf, or upon the place whither he would keep it, behold, upon the morrow, he could not find it, so great was the curse upon the land.

"Wherefore every man did cleave unto that which was his own, with his hands, and would not borrow neither would he lend; and every man kept the hilt of his sword in his right hand, in the defence of his property and his own life and of his wives and children."

After two years Shared's brother "gave battle unto Coriantumr, in which Coriantumr did beat him and did pursue him to the wilderness of Akish. And it came to pass that the brother of Shared did give battle unto him in the wilderness of Akish; and the battle became exceedingly sore, and many thousands fell by the sword."

When mention is made of the heavy loss of life in these wars, it should be remembered that the fighting was hand-to-hand combat with each warrior protecting his own life and surviving only by destroying his opponent.

Once again, Coriantumr lost his kingdom. He "did lay siege to the wilderness; and the brother of Shared did march forth out of the wilderness by night, and slew a part of the army of Coriantumr, as they were drunken. And he came forth to the land of Moron, and placed himself upon the throne of Coriantumr." Meanwhile, "Coriantumr dwelt with his army in the wilderness for the space of two years."

A brother of Shared, whose name was Gilead, now set himself up as king, but "it came to pass that his high priest murdered him as he sat upon his throne."

Then came Lib, "a man of great stature, more than any other man among all the people." He attacked Coriantumr's army and forced it to flee, but in the next encounter, Lib was killed.

Lib's brother Shiz next took arms, and "it came to pass that Shiz pursued after Coriantumr, and he did overthrow many cities, and he did slay both women and children, and he did burn the cities. And there went a fear of Shiz throughout all the land;

yea, a cry went forth throughout the land—Who can stand before the army of Shiz? Behold, he sweepeth the earth before him!"

Shiz was the final great enemy of Coriantumr, the man with whom he fought the last battle. He had "sworn to avenge himself upon Coriantumr of the blood of his brother, who had been slain, and the word of the Lord which came to Ether that Coriantumr should not fall by the sword.

"And thus we see that the Lord did visit them in the fulness of his wrath, and their wickedness and abominations had prepared a way for their everlasting destruction. . . .

"And it came to pass that the people began to flock together in armies, throughout all the face of the land. And they were divided; and a part of them fled to the army of Shiz, and a part of them fled to the army of Coriantumr.

"And so great and lasting had been the war, and so long had been the scene of bloodshed and carnage, that the whole face of the land was covered with the bodies of the dead. And so swift and speedy was the war that there was none left to bury the dead, but they did march forth from the shedding of blood to the shedding of blood, leaving the bodies of both men, women, and children strewed upon the face of the land, to become a prey to the worms of the flesh.

"And the scent thereof went forth upon the face of the land, even upon all the face of the land; wherefore the people became troubled by day and by night, because of the scent thereof."

Ether was commanded of the Lord to observe and record these death throes of the Jaredites, and this he did while hiding "in the cavity of a rock." (Ether 13; 14.)

# Chapter 17

# THE FINAL BATTLE

**W**hile recovering from the wounds of combat, Coriantumr began to remember the words of Ether.

"He saw that there had been slain by the sword already nearly two millions of his people, and he began to sorrow in his heart; yea, there had been slain two millions of mighty men, and also their wives and their children.

"He began to repent of the evil which he had done; he began to remember the words which had been spoken by the mouth of all the prophets, and he saw them that they were fulfiilled thus far, every whit; and his soul mourned and refused to be comforted.

"And it came to pass that he wrote an epistle unto Shiz, desiring him that he would spare the people, and he would give up the kingdom for the sake of the lives of the people.

"And it came to pass that when Shiz had received his epistle he wrote an epistle unto Coriantumr, that if he would give himself up, that he might slay him with his own sword, that he would spare the lives of the people."

The fighting continued. To gain more strength, each army now gathered in all the men, women, and children and made them a part of the total fighting force, putting all the inhabitants on one side or the other.

"Wherefore, they were for the space of four years gathering together the people, that they might get all who were upon the face of the land, and that they might receive all the strength which it was possible that they could receive.

"And it came to pass that when they were all gathered together, every one to the army which he would, with their wives and their children—both men, women and children being armed with weapons of war, having shields, and breastplates, and head-plates, and being clothed after the manner of war—they did march forth one against another to battle; and they fought all that day, and conquered not. . . .

"And it came to pass that on the morrow they did go again to battle, and great and terrible was that day; nevertheless, they conquered not, and when the night came again they did rend the air with their cries, and their howlings, and their mournings, for the loss of the slain of their people."

Seeing the inevitable approaching, Coriantumr "wrote again an epistle unto Shiz, desiring that he would not come again to battle, but that he would take the kingdom, and spare the lives of the people.

"But behold, the Spirit of the Lord had ceased striving with them, and Satan had full power over the hearts of the people; for they were given up unto the hardness of their hearts, and the blindness of their minds that they might be destroyed; wherefore they went again to battle. . . .

"And when the night came they were drunken with anger, even as a man who is drunken with wine; and they slept again upon their swords. And on the morrow they fought again; and when the night came they had all fallen by the sword save it were fifty and two of the people of Coriantumr, and sixty and nine of the people of Shiz."

By the next night there were only thirty-two survivors in Shiz's army and twenty-seven with Coriantumr.

At last only the two leaders remained. "And it came to pass that when they had all fallen by the sword, save it were Coriantumr and Shiz, behold Shiz had fainted with the loss of blood.

"And it came to pass that when Coriantumr had leaned upon his sword, that he rested a little, he smote off the head of Shiz. And it came to pass that after he had smitten off the head of Shiz, that Shiz raised up on his hands and fell; and after that he had struggled for breath, he died.

"And it came to pass that Coriantumr fell to the earth, and became as if he had no life." (Ether 15:1-32.)

Remember that Ether had told Coriantumr that if he would repent, "and all his household, the Lord would give unto him his kingdom and spare the people—otherwise they should be destroyed, and all his household save it were himself. And he should only live to see the fulfilling of the prophecies which had been spoken concerning another people receiving the land for their inheritance; and Coriantumr should receive a burial by them; and every soul should be destroyed save it were Coriantumr." (Ether 13:20-21.)

This was fulfilled. In the book of Omni we read:

"And it came to pass in the days of Mosiah, there was a large stone brought unto him with engravings on it; and he did interpret the engravings by the gift and power of God.

"And they gave an account of one Coriantumr, and the slain of his people. And Coriantumr was discovered by the people of Zarahemla; and he dwelt with them for the space of nine moons.

"It also spake a few words concerning his fathers. And his first parents came out from the tower, at the time the Lord confounded the language of the people; and the severity of the Lord fell upon them according to his judgments, which are just; and their bones lay scattered in the land northward." (Omni 1:20-22.)

# Chapter 18

# THE TWENTY-FOUR PLATES

Ether must have written in great detail, because as Moroni abridged the record, he noted that "the hundredth part I have not written."

At the end of the battle the Lord said to Ether, "Go forth," and as he did, Ether "beheld that the words of the Lord had all been fulfilled." He finished his record and hid the plates, which years later were found by Limhi's people.

"Now the last words which are written by Ether are these: Whether the Lord will that I be translated, or that I suffer the will of the Lord in the flesh, it mattereth not, if it so be that I am saved in the kingdom of God. Amen." (Ether 15:33-34.)

In connection with his abridgment of Ether's plates, Moroni wrote:

"I am commanded that I should hide them up again in the earth.

"Behold, I have written upon these plates the very things which the brother of Jared saw; and there never were greater things made manifest than those which were made manifest unto the brother of Jared.

"Wherefore the Lord hath commanded me to write them; and I have written them. And he commanded me that I should seal them up; and he also hath commanded that I should seal up the interpretation thereof; wherefore I have sealed up the interpreters, according to the commandment of the Lord.

"For the Lord said unto me: They shall not go forth unto the Gentiles until the day that they shall repent of their iniquity, and become clean before the Lord.

"And in that day that they shall exercise faith in me, saith the Lord, even as the brother of Jared did, that they may become sanctified in me, then will I manifest unto them the things which the brother of Jared saw, even to the unfolding unto them all my revelations, saith Jesus Christ, the Son of God, the Father of the heavens and of the earth, and all things that in them are.

"And he that will contend against the word of the Lord, let him be accursed; and he that shall deny these things, let him be accursed; for unto them will I show no greater things, saith Jesus Christ; for I am he who speaketh.

"And at my command the heavens are opened and are shut; and at my word the earth shall shake; and at my command the inhabitants thereof shall pass away, even so as by fire.

"And he that believeth not my words believeth not my disciples; and if it so be that I do not speak, judge ye; for ye shall know that it is I that speaketh, at the last day.

"But he that believeth these things which I have spoken, him will I visit with the manifestations of my Spirit, and he shall know and bear record. For because of my Spirit he shall know that these things are true; for it persuadeth men to do good." (Ether 4:3-11.)

The record not only told the story of the Jaredites but also seems to have covered much of the same history given in the brass plates of Laban, and so Moroni wrote:

"And as I suppose that the first part of this record, which speaks concerning the creation of the world, and also of Adam, and an account from that time even to the great tower, and whatsoever things transpired among the children of men until that time, is had among the Jews—

"Therefore I do not write those things which transpired from the days of Adam until that time; but they are had upon the plates; and whoso findeth them, the same will have power that he may get the full account.

"But behold, I give not the full account, but a part of the account I give, from the tower down until they were destroyed." (Ether 1:3-5.)

# Chapter 19

# MORONI
# ON FAITH

One of the classic passages in the Book of Mormon appears in the twelfth chapter of the book of Ether, written as a commentary on the faith—or lack of it—that Moroni observed among the Jaredites.

Ether had written, "By faith all things are fulfilled." From this Moroni wrote:

"Now, I, Moroni, would speak somewhat concerning these things; I would show unto the world that faith is things which are hoped for and not seen; wherefore, dispute not because ye see not, for ye receive no witness until after the trial of your faith.

"For it was by faith that Christ showed himself unto our fathers, after he had risen from the dead; and he showed not himself unto them until after they had faith in him; wherefore, it must needs be that some had faith in him, for he showed himself not unto the world.

"But because of the faith of men he has shown himself unto the world, and glorified the name of the Father, and prepared a way that thereby others might be partakers of the heavenly gift, that they might hope for those things which they have not seen."

Moroni spoke of the gospel being superior to the law of Moses and explained that "in the gift of his Son hath God prepared a more excellent way; and it is by faith that it hath been fulfilled. For if there be no faith among the children of men God can do no miracle among them; wherefore, he showed not himself until after their faith."

He then went on much as Paul wrote to the Hebrews (Hebrews 11):

"Behold, it was the faith of Alma and Amulek that caused the prison to tumble to the earth.

"Behold, it was the faith of Nephi and Lehi that wrought the change upon the Lamanites, that they were baptized with fire and with the Holy Ghost.

"Behold, it was the faith of Ammon and his brethren which wrought so great a miracle among the Lamanites.

"Yea, and even all they who wrought miracles wrought them by faith, even those who were before Christ and also those who were after.

"And it was by faith that the three disciples obtained a promise that they should not taste of death; and they obtained not the promise until after their faith.

"And neither at any time hath any wrought miracles until after their faith; wherefore they first believed in the Son of God.

"And there were many whose faith was so exceedingly strong, even before Christ came, who could not be kept from within the veil, but truly saw with their eyes the things which they had beheld with an eye of faith, and they were glad."

Speaking of the brother of Jared and his vision of Christ, Moroni wrote: "For the brother of Jared said unto the mountain Zerin, Remove—and it was removed. And if he had not had faith it would not have moved; wherefore thou workest after men have faith."

Moroni also taught this great truth: "Wherefore, ye may also have hope, and be partakers of the gift, if ye will but have faith. Behold it was by faith that they of old were called after the holy order of God."

Addressing the Lord, Moroni wrote:

"Thou hast made us that we could write but little, because of the awkwardness of our hands. Behold, thou hast not made us mighty in writing like unto the brother of Jared, for thou madest him that the things which he wrote were mighty even as thou art, unto the overpowering of man to read them.

"Thou hast also made our words powerful and great, even

that we cannot write them; wherefore, when we write we behold our weakness, and stumble because of the placing of our words; and I fear lest the Gentiles shall mock at our words.

"And when I had said this, the Lord spake unto me, saying: Fools mock, but they shall mourn; and my grace is sufficient for the meek, that they shall take no advantage of your weakness; and if men come unto me I will show unto them their weakness. I give unto men weakness that they may be humble; and my grace is sufficient for all men that humble themselves before me; for if they humble themselves before me, and have faith in me, then will I make weak things become strong unto them.

"Behold, I will show unto the Gentiles their weakness and I will show unto them that faith, hope and charity bringeth unto me—the fountain of all righteousness."

Then came this choice passage:

"For thus didst thou manifest thyself unto thy disciples; for after they had faith, and did speak in thy name, thou didst show thyself unto them in great power.

"And I also remember that thou hast said that thou hast prepared a house for man, yea, even among the mansions of thy Father, in which man might have a more excellent hope; wherefore man must hope, or he cannot receive an inheritance in the place which thou hast prepared.

"And again, I remember that thou has said that thou hast loved the world, even unto the laying down of thy life for the world, that thou mightest take it again to prepare a place for the children of men.

"And now I know that this love which thou hast had for the children of men is charity; wherefore, except men shall have charity they cannot inherit that place which thou hast prepared in the mansions of thy Father.

"Wherefore, I know by this thing which thou hast said, that if the Gentiles have not charity, because of our weakness, that thou wilt prove them, and take away their talent, yea, even that which they have received, and give unto them who shall have more abundantly."

He then closed his writing with these words:

"Now I, Moroni, bid farewell unto the Gentiles, yea, and also unto my brethren whom I love, until we shall meet before the judgment-seat of Christ, where all men shall know that my garments are not spotted with your blood.

"And then shall ye know that I have seen Jesus, and that he hath talked with me face to face, and that he told me in plain humility, even as a man telleth another in mine own language, concerning these things;

"And only a few have I written, because of my weakness in writing.

"And now, I would commend you to seek this Jesus of whom the prophets and apostles have written, that the grace of God the Father, and also the Lord Jesus Christ, and the Holy Ghost, which beareth record of them, may be and abide in you forever. Amen." (Ether 12.)

Thus the record of the Jaredites came to an end.

# THE JAREDITE KINGS

| Reigns of Kings | Other Kings (When Land Was Divided) | Kings in Exile or Captivity |
|---|---|---|
| 1. Jared | | |
| 2. Orihah, son of Jared (righteous king) | | |
| 3. Kib, son of Orihah | | |
| | 4. Corihor, son of Kib | |
| 4. Corihor | | 3. Kib (imprisoned by Corihor) |
| 3. Kib (restored by Shule) | | |
| 5. Shule, son of Kib | | |
| | 6. Noah, son of Corihor | |
| 6. Noah (assassinated by sons of Shule) | | 5. Shule (imprisoned by Noah) |
| 5. Shule (restored by sons; righteous) | 7. Cohor, son of Noah (slain in battle) | |
| 8. Omer, son of Shule | | |
| | 9. Jared, son of Omer (evil) | |
| 9. Jared | | 8. Omer (imprisoned by Jared) |
| 8. Omer (restored by Esrom and Coriantumr) | | |
| 9. Jared (assassinated by Akish) | | 8. Omer (warned in dream and fled to seashore) |
| 10. Akish (evil; killed in battle) | 11. sons of Akish (killed in battle) | |

| Reigns of Kings | Other Kings (When Land Was Divided) | Kings in Exile or Captivity |
|---|---|---|
| 8. Omer | | |
| 12. Emer, son of Omer (righteous) | | |
| 13. Coriantum, son of Emer (righteous) | | |
| 14. Com, son of Coriantum (assassinated by Heth) | | |
| 15. Heth, son of Com (evil; died in famine) | | |
| 16. Shez, son of Heth (righteous) | 17. Shez, son of Shez (killed by robber) | |
| 18. Riplakesh, son of 16. Shez (evil; killed in battle) | | |
| 19. unknown king(s) | 20. Morianton, descendant of Riplakesh | |
| 20. Morianton (evil, but ruled justly) | | |
| 21. Kim, son of Morianton (evil) | | |
| 22. brother of Kim | | 21. Kim (imprisoned by brother) |
| 24. unknown king(s) | | 23. Levi, son of Kim (kept in captivity) |
| 23. Levi (restored by own hand; righteous) | | |
| 25. Corom, son of Levi (righteous) | | |
| 26. Kish, son of Corom | | |

| Reigns of Kings | Other Kings (When Land Was Divided) | Kings in Exile or Captivity |
|---|---|---|
| 27. Lib, son of Kish (righteous) | | |
| 28. Hearthom, son of Lib | | |
| 29. period of unknown kings | | 28. Hearthom (imprisoned by unknown king) |
| | | 30. Heth, son of Hearthom (kept in captivity) |
| | | 31. Aaron, son of Heth (kept in captivity) |
| | | 32. Amnigaddah, son of Aaron (kept in captivity) |
| | | 33. Coriantum, son of Amnigaddah (kept in captivity) |
| | | 34. Com, son of Coriantum |
| 35. Amgid | 34. Com (restored by own hand) | |
| 34. Com (defeated Amgid; righteous) | | |
| 36. Shiblom, son of Com (evil; slain) | 37. brother of Shiblom (evil) | |
| 37. brother of Shiblom or 38. unkown king(s) | | 39. Seth, son of Shiblom |
| 40. Ahah, son of Seth (evil) | | |
| 41. Ethem, son of Ahah (evil) | | |
| 42. Moron, son of Ethem (evil) | 43. unknown warrior | |

| Reigns of Kings | Other Kings (When Land Was Divided | Kings in Exile or Captivity |
| --- | --- | --- |
| 44. unknown warrior, descendant of brother of Jared | | 42. Moron (imprisoned by 44. unknown warrior) |
| 46. unknown king(s) | | 45. Coriantor, son of Moron (kept in captivity) |
| 48. Coriantumr (evil, but repented too late to save people) | | 47. Ether, son of Coriantor (last prophet; lived in hiding) |
| 49. Shared (evil; killed in battle after Coriantumr regained kingdom) | | 48. Coriantumr (imprisoned by Shared) |
| 48. Coriantumr (restored by sons) | | |
| 50. Gilead, brother of Shared (evil; assassinated) | | 48. Coriantumr (dwelt in wilderness) |
| 51. Lib (evil; killed in battle) | 48. Coriantumr (he alone was left alive) | |
| 52. Shiz, brother of Lib (evil; killed in battle) | | |
| the final destruction of the Jaredites | | |

# INDEX

Aaron, 37
Ablom, 40
Adam, 61
Ahah, 50
Air, providing, in barges, 13
Akish, 38-41
Akish, sons of, 40-41
Akish, wilderness of, 55
Alma, 63
America, land of: events on, 19-21; as promised land, 21-23; mighty Gentile nation of, 22-25
Amgid, 37
Ammon, 63
Amnigaddah, 37
Amulek, 63
Animals of Jaredites, 42, 47
Ark, 26-27
Assassination of kings, 35, 40, 46-47, 55, 67-70

Babel, 5-7. *See also* Tower of Babel
Babylon, 6-7
Barges, 13-16, 26-27
Battle, final, of Jaredites, 57-58. *See also* Wars
Blessings for chosen people, 10-11, 42-45
Book of Abraham, 7
Brass plates, 61

Cain, 39
Captivity: of Kib, 34; of Hearthom to Com, 37, 50; of Omer, 38; of Kim and Levi, 44, 49; of last Jaredite kings, 51-52, 54; of kings, 67-70
Charity, 64
Chronology of kings, 67-70
Cohor, 35-36, 53
Com (grandson of Amnigaddah), 37, 50
Com (grandson of Emer), 43, 46

Combinations, secret, 39-40, 46
Coriantor, 51-52
Coriantum (son of Amnigaddah), 37
Coriantum (son of Emer), 43, 46
Coriantumr (last king): Ether prophesies during reign of, 52-54; fights Shared and his brother, 54-55; fights Lib and his brother, Shiz, 55-58; alone remains alive, 59
Coriantumr, (son of Omer), 38
Coriantumr, sons of, 54
Corihor, 34-35, 53
Corom, 44
Creation, 7, 17
Curses, 1, 11, 21, 54-55

Dancing of Jared's daughter, 38-39
Dead, land covered with, 56
Destruction: of Jaredites, 2-4, 54-58; promises of, 23, 31; during reign of Akish, 40-41; during reign of Shiblom, 50; prophecies of complete, 50-51, 54, 59; Ether warns Jaredites of, 52-54
Disciples, three, not to die, 63
Dispersion, divine, 1, 5-6, 10, 12-16

Earth, 19
Eden, 19-20
Emer, 42-43
Epistles between Coriantumr and Shiz, 57-58
Esrom, 38
Ethem, 50
Ether, 4, 52-54, 56-57, 59-60

Faith, 16-17, 52, 62-64
Famines, 46-47, 50
Finger of Lord, 15-17
Flood, 20
Freedom of promised land, 22-23, 30-31